The Films of
SEAN
CONNERY

The Films of
SEAN CONNERY

Emma Andrews

THE CONFUCIAN PRESS, INC.

•

BEAUFORT BOOKS, INC.
New York/Toronto

Heroes of the Movies – Sean Connery

Library of Congress Cataloging in Publication Data

Andrews, Emma.
The films of Sean Connery.

1. Connery, Sean.   I. Title.
PN2287.C585A8   1982   791.43'028'0924   82-12868
ISBN 0-8253-0111-4 (Beaufort Books)

Published in the United States by Beaufort Books, Inc.,
New York, and The Confucian Press, Inc.
Publishing simultaneously in Canada by
General Publishing Co. Limited

Printed in the U.S.A.   First Edition
10 9 8 7 6 5 4 3 2 1

There was a time when I had to prostitute myself to pay the bills. . . the Bond films ended that.'

"I'm a very private person. I always have been," Sean Connery said when announcing that he had married French artist Micheline Roquebrun, but declining to say precisely when the ceremony took place. So it wasn't the years as James Bond that made him wary; it was instinct going way back to the roughest streets in Edinburgh where he was born on August 25, 1930. His father, Joseph Connery, was a removal van driver who never missed a day's work in his life. His mother, Euphamia, worked as a charlady. Sean was the first of their two sons; his younger brother Neil briefly became an actor.

Sean's cot was the bottom drawer of a wardrobe; the lavatory outside on the stairway was shared with twelve other families. Young Sean was a tough little boy, well equipped to keep abreast of the frequent fights in his neighbourhood. "I always enjoyed reading even when I was at school, but I didn't do much of it. I suppose that was partly because of the lack of space at home — four people in a small kitchen in the evenings. It's just not easy to settle down with a book."

The leisure activities of his childhood were playing street football, extremely well from all accounts, and occasional visits to the local cinema when there was enough money (although an empty jam jar sometimes gained admittance when there was not). Westerns and adventure films were the favourites, and following the exploits of Flash Gordon.

As a child he'd go to the municipal baths where the payment of 3d, 6d or a shilling governed how much water he could luxuriate in with his piece of carbolic soap the size of a domino. "I think much hardship is perceived only in retrospect. You don't think of yourself as underprivileged if you have nothing to compare your condition with. You don't miss holidays, for example, because they're not even in your fantasies. In those days it was never a question of

Opposite: in a BBC television production of Anna Karenina

one's ambitions. It was the struggle of going from day to day that counted."

The canny aggression which for some years was submerged under the gloss of James Bond is easy to understand: when you grow up in a grim neighbourhood, without any spare cash, it is difficult to completely shake off scepticism. He has always maintained: "There's nothing special about being an actor. It's a job, like being a carpenter or a bricklayer, and I've never stopped being amazed at the mystique people attach to my business." As somebody once said: Sean Connery is a serious man in a world of tinsel. A man with a deep contempt for shoddiness ("The pleasure of work comes in the meshing of dozens of professional skills — that's what it's all about. I hate bunglers more than anything") and a personal philosophy to "Leave no place worse than it was when you arrived. And if you can make it better do it."

By the age of nine he had a milk round to augment the family coffers and he left school at thirteen. At fifteen he joined the Royal Navy as a gunner in an anti-aircraft carrier squadron. After four years he was invalided out with ulcers. Returning to civilian life he had a succession of temporary jobs — lorry driver, cement mixer, bricklayer, steel bender, printer's devil, lifeguard, coffin polisher.

His fierce loyalty to Scotland was clearly defined and would grow, and his right arm bears the tattooed legend "Scotland Forever" and "Mum and Dad" (he apparently thought of adding "Death before Dishonour" since that is the code he lives by). When he became James Bond the tattoos had to be carefully shielded: they were hardly the image for the superspy of the '60s.

For a time he considered a career in commercial art and to finance a course he divided his time at the Edinburgh School of Art between study and

Opposite: in
Hell Drivers

modelling (he posed, invariably, as either a Greek athlete or a Roman warrior). He was also keen on body building and it was a journey to London to enter a Mr Universe competition which indirectly led to his first stage role. While in London he met a friend who was in the chorus of "South Pacific". The friend told Connery that another member of the chorus had recently left and they were looking for a replacement. Connery auditioned and no one was more surprised than he was when he was selected. "The idea of touring round the country was what appealed to me. I didn't seriously consider myself as an actor. I told them I'd done a lot of work in Scottish rep I hadn't actually, but it's pretty hard to check." The next forty-eight hours were spent taking intensive private lessons so that his dancing deficiency wouldn't be spotted.

He stayed with the show for two years. When the show arrived in Manchester he was asked if he would consider playing football for Manchester United. Turning it down was his first commitment to an acting career. "My parents weren't horrified that I had become an actor. I shouldn't think they felt anything, or if they did, they were glad I'd found something to do. You see I wasn't really qualified to do anything." After six months with the show he became fascinated by the acting and volunteered to understudy some of the speaking roles. He caught up on his reading and gained confidence. Enough confidence to know at the end of the show's touring commitments that he'd had enough experience in the chorus and should be moving on. Despite the necessary salary cut involved he elected to join a small suburban repertory company outside London where he would have the chance of playing bigger roles.

He played the battered fighter on the skids, Mountain McClintock, in the BBC television production of "Requiem for a Heavyweight" in 1956 after Jack

Opposite: in
Another Time
Another Place

Palance, the producer's first choice, was forced to cancel. It was a splendid production and made a great number of people take notice of Connery.

Unlike many actors who for years make tiny, uncredited appearances in films (for example Michael Caine and Oliver **Reed**), Sean Connery's screen debut was a credited appearance resulting from his work in television. The film was *No Road Back*, a taut little thriller about a blind and deaf lady who acted as a fence for the criminals who used her London club as their hideout. Directed by Montgomery Tully, it was recognised as being good of its kind, although some critics pondered over the amount of brutality. But it is unarguably true that it was not until the James Bond films that Sean Connery's potential was finally given the scope it demanded, even if it ultimately blinkered that potential. Until then the films he made offered little opportunity for him to shine and it was in television that his reputation grew.

As a result of "Requiem for a Heavyweight", 20th Century-Fox signed him to a long-term contract and promptly forgot to use him (although, before casting Curt Jurgens in *The Inn of the Sixth Happiness* they had considered casting Connery in the role). Fox mainly loaned him out during his contract days, and it wasn't until 1962 that they put him amid all the other stars in *The Longest Day*.

In 1957 he gave an uncredited performance in *Hell Drivers*, directed by C Raker Endfield (later to be known as Cy Endfield) with a script by John Kruse and the director. It exposed the workings of a particular road haulage firm where the hero, Tom, played by Stanley Baker, was in fierce competition with the foreman, Red, played by Patrick McGoohan, who was the peacemaker and champion driver of the company. The film ended in a life or death struggle and one critic noted that it would be of archival interest to anyone wanting to know about

Opposite: with Janet Munro in Darby O'Gill and the Little People

road haulage in the '50s. The performances were praised although the story was unconvincingly shallow.

In *Time Lock* (also 1957) Connery gave another unbilled appearance in a drama about a boy locked in a bank vault during the weekend. The tension of the situation was increased by the knowledge that the oxygen in the vault would not be sufficient. Based on a television play by Arthur Hailey, whose later novels "Hotel", "Airport" and "Wheels" made fine screen entertainment, *Time Lock* showed its origins while achieving a degree of tension.

Action of the Tiger was a melodrama about a mysterious Frenchwoman who visits Athens and persuades an adventurer (played by Van Johnson) to smuggle her into Albania where her brother is a political prisoner. Connery's next film, *Another Time, Another Place*, was no more convincing, although it gave him a bigger slice of the celluloid cake. He played a BBC war correspondent who has an affair with an American journalist (played by Lana Turner). When he is killed she visits his home town and becomes friendly with his wife and children who, after initial resentment, come to view her more kindly when she says that although he was the love of her life he never regarded her as more than a passing attraction.

For the Walt Disney organisation Sean Connery joined Janet Munro in *Darby O'Gill and the Little People*, based on the H T Kavanagh "Darby O'Gill" stories. Directed by Disney veteran Robert Stevenson it was pleasant fare set in Ireland and was a combination of love, laughter and leprechauns.

Tarzan's Greatest Adventure (1959) was directed by John Guillermin with Gordon Scott as Tarzan and Anthony Quayle as the baddie, Slade. Slade, a would-be diamond robber, is hotly pursued by Tarzan who has lovely Angie (Sara Shane), a plane crash

Opposite: with Janet Munro in Darby O'Gill and the Little People

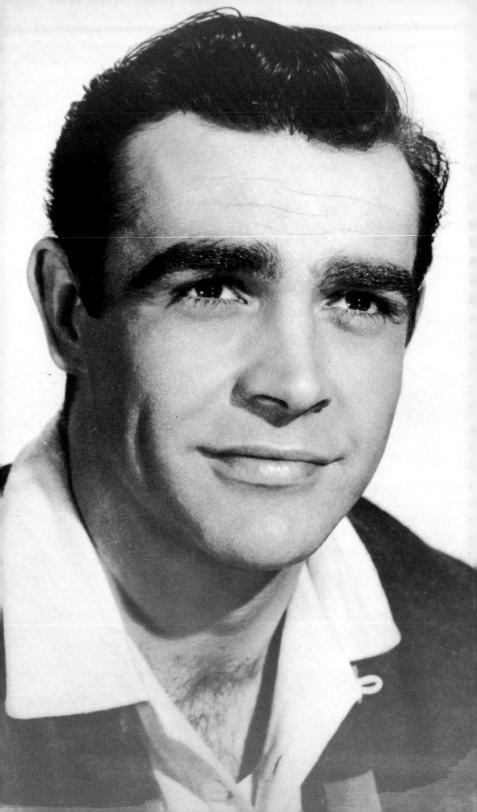

survivor, in tow for the duration.

The Frightened City (1961) gave Sean Connery third billing in a film about a protection racket in London which begins when a crooked accountant attempts to amalgamate six gangs using a burglar, Paddy (Sean Connery), to collect the money. It was a successful thriller with a plausible background and generally all aspects seemed to please, particularly the direction and the laconically humorous script.

On the Fiddle (1961) was Connery's first film with top billing as Pascoe, a slow-witted gypsy helping wide boy Pope (Alfred Lynch) to operate a lucrative racket in the RAF which will enable them to avoid the fighting war. Eventually they are forced into a skirmish but emerge unscathed and are lavishly decorated for heroism. Connery was praised for his performance as the ideal foil for the quick witted Pope.

He then made his first and only film for 20th-Century Fox — five years into his contract with them. It was a cameo in *The Longest Day*, an unbilled performance as Private Flanagan, a tough seasoned veteran soldier whose Irish temperament sees him through the landings at Juno Beach. The film, with its gargantuan cast and high ideals, was based on the book by Cornelius Ryan. Various directors contributed their segments, and various actors theirs.

Meanwhile, on November 30, 1962 Sean Connery married actress Diane Cilento, a union that was never less than explosive but which lasted off and on for eleven years. They had one son, Jason, and Diane Cilento also has a daughter, Giovanna, from her first marriage. Looking back on the marriage, Connery said: "One is always reluctant to admit failure, and a marriage that goes wrong is as bad as anything can be." He was, however, devoted to the children, and his son now lives with him.

In the late '50s Connery was recognised by the fan

Opposite: in Darby O'Gill and the Little People

magazines as a potential superstar. Although he escaped any set mould, his virile good looks, more American than British, clearly marked him as an actor worth watching. But the roles scarcely matched the potential. Interviewed in "Picturegoer" at that time he pondered the success of stars like Alan Ladd who needed to stand on a box to maintain level pegging with his leading ladies during love scenes. "What they need is someone like me," said Connery. Again it was television which provided the spur to his film career. In 1961 he starred opposite Claire Bloom in "Anna Karenina" and it caused a great stir with the public.

Happily this coincided with the world-wide search for an actor to play James Bond. Among the famous actors considered were Trevor Howard, Richard Burton, James Mason and Peter Finch. Unknowns, too, stood in line, among them the little-known Sean Connery. The producers might have settled for any one of the famous names but the author, Ian Fleming, had final say. He chose Connery. That decision meant that, for Connery, the supporting roles were over. He had played the game for the highest stakes and he had won. It was the turning point of his film career.

Bondage began with *Dr No* and continued for a decade. It assumed lunatic proportions. "You can't explain to anybody what these pressures subject you to because most people haven't experienced it," says Connery. "If I went into a public place I did so completely at my own risk and you can't complain about your privacy being infringed upon. But on the other hand I made myself go into some places and move around because you can very easily have a Burton–Taylor situation, which is greatly self-provoked, where you have a phalanx of guards in the restaurant in front of you, setting up the scene like a tableau before you enter."

Dr No, produced by later Bond standards on a

Opposite: in Frightened City

miniscule budget, was a calculated risk. It proved a phenomenon. Bernard Lee as Bond's boss, 'M', and Lois Maxwell as Bond's faithful secretary Miss Moneypenny, little realised that they would be trotted out year after year for subsequent Bond epics. None of them recognised at the time the kind of mania that would later surround the films. Connery least of all.

Although the faults of *Dr No* are evident, it has a freshness, a humour and a gloss which was and remains original. Connery's Bond was exceptionally good although critics carped that he wasn't the ideal actor for Fleming's smooth spy. Since Fleming had the final say in the selection, that criticism scarcely holds up. Such reservations were certainly not held by the public and the film's reputation grew steadily. The scene for which the film will long be remembered is that of Ursula Andress rising, Venus like, from the sea, dressed in a white bikini. It was a spectacular advertisement for bikinis — although it looks modest by today's standards — and made Ursula Andress a star. A trick which worked for later Bond ladies, but not for as many as the publicity would have you believe.

Once the legend was spawned, the repercussions would be endless. At the time Connery was confident that Bond would not prove a chain. "I'm asked if I'm worried about getting tagged as Bond. I suppose I would have been if I hadn't done a lot of other things." Over the next decade he would not be so sure.

Connery was paid £15,000 for *Dr No*. Business began in a small way. Connery himself confessed that he was more interested in Ian Fleming as a person that in the character he had created. In fact, he had only read two of the James Bond novels. "The director, Terence Young, and I worked hard on the character to get in some humour: it certainly isn't in the books I

Opposite: a tiny appearance in The Longest Day

have read." The humour was a welcome addition an‹
Connery, seemingly completely at home in the guis‹
of the sophisticated spy, absorbed and became part o‹
the myths and folklore that grew up around this mos‹
popular of celluloid spies. The demarcation line
became blurred: who knew in the end whether it wa‹
Connery or Bond who preferred vodka martini
shaken but not stirred? Was it the fictional characte‹
who played golf, or was it Connery himself?
The second Bond, *From Russia With Love*, followed ‹
year later, in 1963. Robert Shaw made a menacin‹
villain and Lotte Lenya was the female oppositio‹
while Daniela Bianchi looked fetching as the heroine‹
Connery shot his cuffs, demolished his assailants an‹
wooed his ladies with devastating aplomb and th‹
public went wild with delight. Producers Cubb‹
Broccoli and Harry Saltzman must have realise‹
about then that they were sitting on something‹
eminently bankable and the budgets increase‹
accordingly on the feasible theory that the more yo‹
put into the product the more you get out of it. As fa‹
as Bond was concerned — as long as Connery wa‹
playing him — the theory was sound.
Sean Connery, beginning to chaff a little at the‹
limitations, but not yet completely disenchanted,
departed from Bond to make *Woman of Straw* fo‹
producer Michael Relph and director Basil Dearden,
Starring Gina Lollobrigida and Ralph Richardson‹
(Connery's favourite actor) it had Connery in a‹
grossly unsympathetic part as the nephew of a wealth‹
old despot (Richardson) who plots his uncle's demise‹
with the reluctant co-operation of the old man's nurse‹
(Lollobrigida). It all turns out disastrously because‹
the nurse isn't really keen to help, particularly when‹
the old man dies suddenly after making a new wil‹
leaving her everything. The police naturally haul her‹
off but the nephew's hand in the events finally‹

becomes known.

Initially there were clashes between Miss Lollobrigida and Connery on the set. Apparently she arrived late on her first day and immediately started telling director Basil Dearden how her scenes should be shot. Connery instantly put a stop to that: "Either he is directing the picture or you are directing it. If it's you I may not be in it." Lollobrigida backed off and after that there was harmony.

The film was generally felt to need a touch of Hitchcock's skill in making the menace work and Connery was to experience exactly that on his next film, *Marnie*. Now a cult Hitchcock film, it was to have been Grace Kelly's return from retirement. In the event Hitchcock's latest discovery 'Tippi' Hedren (from *The Birds*) played the Grace Kelly part. Hitchcock sent Connery a story outline and seemed surprised when he asked to read the script before commiting himself. Connery, who had been trapped that way before, insisted, but agreed to make the film once he had seen the script.

Marnie ('Tippi' Hedren) is a compulsive thief who moves from town to town changing her identity and appearance each time, convincing her boss of her reliability before making off with the contents of the safe. Without friends, without ties she continues her life of crime and between appointments she visits the only two creatures she loves — her crippled mother and her horse. Thunderstorms and bright red colours have an unsettling effect on Marnie but the reasons for this we don't discover until the end of the picture. In the interim her plan to rob the safe of her latest employer is foiled when the boss (Sean Connery) falls in love with her and threatens her with exposure to the police or marriage. *Marnie* is much celebrated in some quarters and Hitchcock's brilliant camera plotting remains classic although the inexperience of Miss Hedren in such a complex role did not add to the film.

Opposite: an action scene from Dr No

After *Marnie* came the third James Bond film, *Goldfinger*, a favourite with many people and the most expensive thus far, it starred Honor Blackman as Pussy Galore, Gert Frobe as the villainous Goldfinger and Shirley Eaton, who received acres of publicity for a performance lasting very few minutes, culminating with her being totally covered in gold paint.

Away from Bond, Connery made one of his finest films, Sidney Lumet's *The Hill*. Oswald Morris' photography in stark black and white contributed to the claustrophobic atmosphere inherent in this brutal story of a North African detention camp for would be deserters in World War II. The title referred to the punishment frequently used when the men were forced to struggle with full packs over a man-made hill under the broiling sun. Ian Hendry was superb as the sadistic Staff Sergeant Williams who punishes and torments the prisoners beyond human endurance. Connery as one of the prisoners gave a remarkable performance of a man under unendurable stress. Brutal, savage and not always comprehensible (in America subtitles were given to help audiences with the porridge-thick accents), the film's raw drama was utterly compelling. Lumet turned in a powerful movie, stimulating his cast into unforgettable performances. It was to be the first of several films Connery and Lumet would make together.

Connery saw *The Hill* again recently and commented that the soundtrack was bad, too realistic to be acceptable. But he feels the film was probably ahead of its time. Certainly the public were not ready to take Connery in this un-Bondlike guise.

Back to Bond for *Thunderball* and for the first time hints of Connery's dissatisfaction with the films crept into the performance. His humour and expression seemed to mirror the growing antagonism he felt toward the character. It was distinguished by some

Opposite: in From Russia with Love

fine underwater sequences but although these scenes were admirable they slowed down the action and the film was one of the least memorable Bond pictures. As usual, a fair supply of female form was on view — Claudine Auger, Luciana Paluzzi, Martine Beswick, Mollie Peters and the invincible Lois Maxwell, the only Bond lady to stay the course.

Connery made another departure from Bond to play a dotty poet opposite Joanne Woodward and Jean Seberg in Irvin Kershner's *A Fine Madness*, based on the novel by Elliott Baker. The film succeeded in showing a poet who really works at his job and Miss Woodward was widely praised for her performance as the wife who copes with a poet husband.

Another return to Bond for *You Only Live Twice*, shot largely on location in Japan where Connery, unhappier than ever, was subjected to rampant Bond mania from Japanese fans. The film was well up to par with more gadgets than ever — an escalating feature of the films which the producers, incredibly managed to continue capping. It was after this that Connery severed his association with Bond and the search began to find a substitute.

When pressed — since it is not a subject he enjoys discussing — Sean Connery acknowledges that it was Bond which made him wealthy, helping him to achieve his goals. But it was also an effective blocking device between him and a wider acting experience.

As the popularity of the Bond films accelerated, so Connery's personal disenchantment grew. Discussing the films' producers, Saltzman and Broccoli, in an interview with The Guardian, Connery said: "They're not exactly enamoured of one another. Probably because they're both sitting on fifty million dollars or pounds and looking across the desk at each other thinking, 'That bugger's got half of what should be all mine'." James Bond became Connery's personal Frankenstein. All the time he was starring in the

Opposite: in From Russia with Love

Bond films, the public was reluctant to accept him in any other role. Several fine films were the scapegoats. Connery then made his first western, *Shalako*, directed by Edward Dmytryk and shot on location in Spain. It was widely advertised as the first British western and the cast certainly substantiated that claim — Stephen Boyd, Jack Hawkins, Honor Blackman, Eric Sykes. But the leading lady could in no way be called British — Brigitte Bardot. The press went wild — Connery and Bardot, together! It was bound to be inflammable. Actually it wasn't and the speculation on the location linked Bardot and Stephen Boyd much more than Bardot and Connery. As a western hero Connery was very effective.

To America next for Martin Ritt's homage to the Pennsylvania miners of the late 19th Century, *The Molly Maguires*. With Richard Harris and Sean Connery in the leading roles the film exposed the sombre hopelessness of the miners' lot but the final impression was bleakly punishing.

The Red Tent was an Italian–Russian co-production with an all star cast and took two years to make. Peter Finch starred as General Nobile and Connery was the explorer Amundsen who set out to rescue Nobile and his crew after their dirigible crash-landed in the Arctic. Nobile was accused of abandoning his comrades and the film fantasised a trial where each member of the crew tells the story from his point of view. Connery, made up to appear an old man, and Finch, emerged with some credit, but the film was overlong and exceedingly dull although Ennio Morricone's fine music helped alleviate boredom.

The Anderson Tapes, Connery's second film with Sidney Lumet, was far better. A taut, exciting thriller which looked at bugging long before Watergate and *The Conversation* made it the latest fascination, it starred Dyan Cannon as Connery's leading lady. Connery played an ex-convict who plots a

Opposite: as James Bond in Goldfinger

recision-timed robbery.

When Sean Connery abandoned James Bond, the producers, Saltzman and Broccoli, convinced that Bond would outlive Connery's contribution, bravely went ahead with former male model George Lazenby. The resulting *On Her Majesty's Secret Service* was a pale shadow. Connery can afford to be generous and says that the responsibility was not wholly Lazenby's. But the producers were even more anxious to lure Connery back. The offers got bigger and bigger and finally Connery agreed to make *Diamonds Are Forever*. The deal has been called the best any actor has ever wrung out of a company since the days of Mary Pickford. As well as a gigantic fee for doing the film, Connery would be allowed to make two further films of his choice for United Artists. In addition he had a percentage and a clause in his contract which meant that if the film overran its eighteen-week schedule, he would be paid a further 10,000 dollars a week. "It can be done if there's money at stake," said Connery. "I admire efficiency; like watching a good racehorse, or the way Picasso works — where everything functions perfectly within its capacity. But, talking to some of these moguls about it is like trying to describe to someone who has never taken exercise what it feels like to feel fit when you do exercise. They don't understand."

This anti-establishment attitude does not extend to film units. Connery is enormously popular with film technicians: he never throws his weight around and he always treats everyone with respect. He seems to regard himself as a member of the crew and — perhaps because of his background — he seems more comfortable with technicians, electricians, grips and gaffers than with the movie brass. He uses his fame and power to get what he wants from the front office, but when he's working it's almost as if he is unaware of both.

Opposite: in Goldfinger

34

In *Diamonds are Forever* the old enthusiasm was bac
and no tell-tale boredom showed — at that f
boredom would be churlish. The contrast between
and the ill-fated *On Her Majesty's Secret Servi*
helped make *Diamonds Are Forever* a gigant
box-office success. Much of the film was shot c
location in Las Vegas and Jill St John and Lana Woc
were the ladies.

Connery's fee went straight to The Scotti
International Educational Trust which he helpe
form and of which he is still Vice-Chairman. Its aim
are, "the advancement of education for the publ
benefit and the provision of facilities for recreatic
and other leisure time activities."

Says Connery: "The provocation was why so man
Scots had to get out of Scotland. We decided the be
thing to do was not to try to find out why they left bu
to stimulate interest so they wanted to stay. It
investment in people as much as anything. Its purpos
is really to narrow the cultural gap in Scotland — an
it is a very wide one. Actually, it involves variou
things as they come up. We sent a young pianist t
Vienna. We have done an impartial survey on th
Clydeside problems. We've set up a chair of drama a
Strathclyde University."

Scottish nationalism is vitally important to Sea
Connery and he became an ardent supporter of th
Scottish National Party, even considering standing fo
Parliament in 1969. "I'm in favour of fragmentation i
general. I don't believe in the Common Market, i
the United States or in the Soviet Union — becaus
there'll always be national differences and skirmishes
and the world's in a highly dangerous situation whe
it splits up into three uncontrollable superpowers. S
Scotland should pull away somewhat after hundred
of years of taking second place to England. The sac
thing is the indifference of the Scottish electorate —
more than 60 percent of which didn't bother to vot

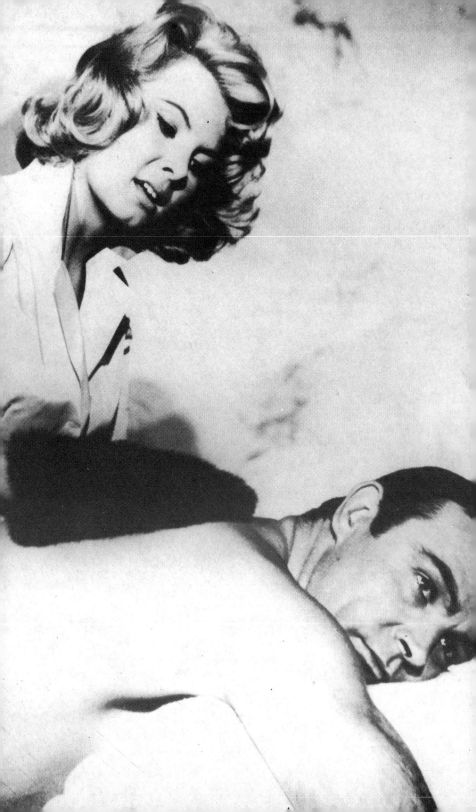

hen given the choice of devolution."

he first film under his deal with United Artists was
he Offence, directed by Sidney Lumet, based on
ohn Hopkins' play "This Story of Yours" which was
 big success at the Royal Court Theatre in London. It
as made for Connery's production company,
'antallon Films (the name has no particular
gnificance to Connery — he saw it somewhere and
10ught it attractive — but since then he has
iscovered that it's the name of an old sailing ship and
 castle outside Edinburgh). *The Offence* told of a
oliceman of many years service who has gradually
ecome disgusted and corrupted by the horrendous
ights he has witnessed over the years. Arresting a
uspected child molester (Ian Bannen), the
oliceman goes berserk and the film ponders the
uestion of whether policemen can stay immune from
1e criminality they observe. Connery's performance
10wed the disintegration of a man, tortured by his
wn inhibitions and prejudices. A fine supporting cast
1cluded Trevor Howard, Vivien Merchant, Peter
3owles. "We rehearsed with John Hopkins before we
tarted shooting," said Connery. "In my experience it
vas the first time everything has meshed together so
vell." His involvement on the production side of the
ilm led to his wholehearted promotion of it and the
ress were treated to a co-operative and genial star.
Ie hadn't particularly enjoyed the production side
10wever. "There was more to it than I'd imagined,"
1e told me at the time. "I was the new boy and it was
ery strange. Obviously I've got a lot to learn. I kept
vanting to get on with making the film and I found I
lidn't really like the other side of the business."
or some years he pondered over the second film
inder the deal. The main reason was the dearth of
;ood scripts. "Finding a good property is always a
>roblem. The big companies have the habit of buying
ıp the best sellers to stop another company getting

Opposite: in
Thunderball

hold of them so when you decide you want to do there's already a huge price on it. Whenever peopl offer me a script I ask what money is against it becaus I've been caught before saying 'that's marvellous' to script and then discovering that buying it woul capsize the budget."

One of his keenest ambitions at the time was to mak a film of "The Devil Drives" which told th fascinating story of explorer Sir Richard Burton. H was offered the part some years earlier but the director John Frankenheimer acquired it and offere the role to Alan Bates. Since then the property ha once more become available but the scope of th book would necessitate lavish locations — Turke India and other far-flung global haunts. The budg would have to be gigantic. He was also intent o making a version of "Macbeth" but Roman Polanski production for Playboy meant that the idea had to b shelved. He has directed on the stage — the West En production of "I've Seen You Cut Lemons" — an toys with the possibility of writing and directing fo the screen. He has little desire to return to the stage a an actor: "I don't have the sort of compulsion tha makes me want to go on night after night."

Connery wears affluence warily. You sense that h has not shaken loose the memories of a impoverished youth. He has become a shrew investor, according to one financier friend, and is ver good with his money. In 1975 he helped found a Pa Mall Merchant Bank, and is not only clever bu careful, sharing the Scottish aversion to lavishness He will pay for his round of drinks, but he expect everyone else to do so too.

In fact it was a documentary about the problems o the Upper Clyde shipbuilders which he directed, *Th Bowler and the Bunnet*, that stimulated him toward the formation of the Scottish Internationa Educational Trust. "What that film did for me ir

Opposite: in Thunderball

personal terms was to make me realise that part of me belonged to that kind of background. I thought I'd left it all behind me. I thought I'd been liberated from that John Knoxian, narrow environment. I had in a way, but I just couldn't turn my back on it completely."

His devotion to Scotland is manifested in many ways, one of them being his obsession for the country's traditional sport, golf. He learned to play for *Goldfinger* and found that he enjoyed the game. Now his handicap is down to six and he plays as frequently as possible. "Golf is a loner's game: it had to be a Scottish invention," he says, admitting, when pressed, "I'm a loner. I've never been in any groups for long. I believe conglomerates and groups are highly dangerous." His golf clubs are his most constant travelling companion and wherever he is in the world his first requirement is locating the best golf links in the vicinity. Making *A Bridge Too Far* in Holland during 1976 he practised between takes and spent every available morning or afternoon off challenging the local professionals to a round. When there isn't a golf course handy, he also plays a mean tennis game, coached by his good friend Lew Hoad.

After *The Offence* Connery made John Boorman's science fiction film *Zardoz*. The film which Boorman produced, directed and wrote, cast Connery as Zed in a world of the future where the intelligentsia have secured themselves in a Vortex leaving the wild masses to forage for themselves in the Outlands. Zed, an Outlands strongman, manages to get inside the Vortex and as the outsider is an object of great interest. Ultimately he brings down the preferred society. Connery went into the film when Burt Reynolds was forced to withdraw for health reasons. Charlotte Rampling co-starred and the film was shot on ravishing locations in Ireland. Some critics complained of the simplistic theory which was basic

Opposite: in You Only Live Twice

science fiction but cleverly dressed up. Geoffrey Unsworth's photography helped the film look exquisite.

Connery went to Norway to make *Ransom* for director Casper Wrede. A modern thriller about hijacking and its prevention, it also starred Ian McShane. The film is set in Amsterdam where a gang of Japanese terrorists have kidnapped the French Ambassador and are holding him prisoner in his own embassy demanding an enormous ransom and a Boeing as means of escape. Connery played the head of security who determines that the terrorists will not succeed. While making the film in Norway Connery dined with a friend at the Continental Hotel in Oslo. A little old lady approached the table and asked the friend: "Is that James Bond you're dining with?" The friend replied: "Well, I'm eating with Sean Connery." The lady's disappointment was obvious. "Oh, he looks like James Bond," she said. Connery's reaction to the incident is not recorded, but he has mellowed with the years and the early truculence has become less in evidence, though he simmers close to the surface. "There was a time when I had to prostitute myself to pay the bills. At least I am thankful to the Bond films for ending that. The money was good and I needed it then. As the world fever mounted I got scared and thought more and more about how I could pull out. I quit at the right moment both for myself and the Bond producers."

He played a small part in Sidney Lumet's star-studded *Murder on the Orient Express*, based on the thriller by Agatha Christie. With Albert Finney as Hercule Poirot, the rest of the cast was a glossary of the legendary names of cinema and theatre — Lauren Bacall, Ingrid Bergman, Jacqueline Bisset, John Gielgud, Wendy Hiller, Anthony Perkins, Vanessa Redgrave, Richard Widmark and Michael York. Connery played Indian Army Colonel Arbuthnott.

Opposite: in The Molly Maguires

He went to Spain for *The Wind and the Lion* directed by John Milius and co-starring Candice Bergen and Brian Keith. The film was set in Tangier and America at the turn of the century. Connery was the leader of a group of bandits who kidnap Mrs Eden Pedecaris (Candice Bergen), an aristocratic American, and her two children. The Government intervention to get her back even involves the President of the United States, Theodore Roosevelt (Brian Keith) who comes to respect the wild man he never meets. In captivity there grows a grudging attraction between abductor and abducted. "Beautifully played with cool wit by both Connery and Candice Bergen, and supplied with dialogue which rings like a rapier duel as each probes to uncover weaknesses and discovers strengths."

The swashbuckling strain continued in *The Man Who Would Be King*, based on the Rudyard Kipling short story, directed by John Huston. Huston had wanted to make it for decades — Clark Gable and Humphrey Bogart were going to make it when Bogie died — but finally it was Michael Caine as Peachy Carnehan and Sean Connery as Daniel Dravot, two ex-British army sergeants, circa 1880, in the primitive Indian country of Kafiristan who get carried away when the locals believe they are kings. Michael Caine remembers it as the best relationship he ever enjoyed with another actor. "At the beginning we didn't know how the relationship between Sean and me would work out. The two of us sat down and discussed the whole thing very thoroughly, since we are both down-to-earth people. We realised early on that we could play it as two actors fighting each other with one trying to edge the other out and get the close ups ... or we could play it by walking round and round and bringing each other into close up for the most interesting lines, to improve the picture. We both agreed that we wanted an improved picture."

It was during the making of *The Man Who Would Be*

Opposite: in Martin Ritt's The Molly Maguires

King in Morocco that Sean Connery announced he had married Micheline Roquebrun four months earlier in Casablanca. More specific he would not be. Micheline, an intelligent, sexy redhead is an accomplished painter, talented cook and widely admired by the locals in Marbella where the couple live with Sean's son, Jason, and Micheline's son' Stefan. Their legal residence is Monte Carlo where they have an apartment, but it is the villa in Marbella with its eleven golf courses in the immediate vicinity and, should that pall, the Mediterranean which is their retreat. "My home is like a hospital," Sean says. "It's where I go to recover." The beautiful people who frequent Marbella try to prise the Connerys into their gatherings, but succeed only rarely. One hostess comments: "Dozens of beautiful women make themselves available, but Sean doesn't allow himself to be pursued, he doesn't give them a chance. I think he and Micheline are a very happy couple."

Similarly he has never succumbed to lucrative offers to write his life story on the grounds that he would never be allowed to suffer amnesia at the bedroom door. "I could certainly write some strong stuff, but I don't think I would feel too comfortable in my own skin. You can't write those private things without other people getting hurt."

Sometimes he articulates his worries for his son and stepson; "My problem was poverty. Theirs is being the sons of a film star. It is something they will have to negotiate and learn to handle. They'll not easily have the drive that a hard early life supposedly supplies, but that can't be imposed. All one can do is give them the best education — in the fullest sense of the word — and hope for the best."

With scarcely a day off after *The Man Who Would Be King*, Connery began work on *Robin and Marian*, Richard Lester's view of the Robin Hood legend, showing them in their declining years when Robin

Opposite: with Hardy Kruger in The Red Tent

inally returns disillusioned from the Crusades. It marked the return to the screen of Audrey Hepburn and very welcome that was. The film was generally liked and Connery was singled out as "probably the most improved British actor of the decade" by Films Illustrated. Or as a friend, publicist turned producer Quinn Donoghue put it: "He went from a nude model to a chorus boy to an accidental star without major training. There's no reason why he should be the fine actor he is."

Connery went to Ireland to make *The Next Man* for Richard Sarafian, a thriller with Connery playing a Saudi-Arabian minister involved in a scheme to break the influence of the United States and the Soviet Union in the Middle East. Connery emerged with some reasonable notices, though the film itself went largely unnoticed.

Almost immediately he travelled to Holland to join Richard Attenborough's cast of superstars for *A Bridge Too Far*. Connery played Major General Robert Urquhart, commander of the British First Airborne Division in this epic version of Operation Market Garden, Field Marshal Montgomery's plan of September 1944 aimed at ending the war by Christmas. The real General Urquhart was present during filming on the original landing zones near Arnhem and when he was asked how he felt about Sean Connery portraying him he confessed he wasn't much of a filmgoer and hadn't heard of Connery before. "But my wife and daughter had just seen a film of his — I think it was *The King and I*," said the good General (obviously meaning *The Man Who Would Be King*). "They told me — 'He'll do!'"

Meteor was the disaster movie without which no actor's filmography would seem to be complete. Connery was the hero of the hour, trying to avert catastrophe when the world is threatened with total destruction in seven days. Ronald Neame directed,

Opposite: in
The Red Tent

but, as one critic put it "never comes close to convincing that — as Bradley (Connery) predicts in the event of the meteor landing — a new Ice Age is at hand."

Much more fun was to be had from *The First Great Train Robbery*, a stylish Victorian caper directed by Michael Crichton which was, tragically, the last film completed by master cinematographer Geoffrey Unsworth. Connery was a gentleman crook, Lesley Anne Down his stunning mistress, Donald Sutherland an Irish safe cracker. It was a delightful robbery and Connery, thatched and bearded, came in for his fair share of the kudos.

Cuba reunited Connery with his *Robin and Marian* director, Richard Lester, and bearing in mind the lack of audience response to this literate tale of the crumbling Batista regime of the late '50s in Cuba, he might have done well to avoid the experience. Mind you, co-star Brooke Adams, playing his mistress, had nothing but praise for Connery. "I have never met an actor like him," she says. "Most actors like to keep secret what they do and how they do it. Not Sean. He taught me a lot about how to psychologise a character. He left the room and walked in like three different men, simply by altering his relationship to space: the difference was incredible. But mostly I'm in awe of his never trying to inspire awe."

Connery was philosophical: "I have done more than my fair share of films which didn't succeed at the box office."

When the Monty Python team were setting up *Time Bandits*, they decided in a fit of optimistic madness to ask Sean Connery to play King Agamemnon. They tracked him down to a golf course (where else?) and he told them he had a few days free before he began work on *Outland*. If *Time Bandits* could fit in with his schedule he'd do it.

Connery's scenes were largely with a young eleven

Opposite: with Dyan Cannon in The Anderson Tapes

ar old Craig Warnock, overwhelmed to find himself

e centre of attention in Morocco's furnace heat with
vast crowd of technicians and Sean Connery.
irector Terry Gilliam is vocal in praise of Connery.
He was great. He suggested ways of shooting around
e scene to get his sequences done and then
concentrate on Craig afterwards. He simplified it for
e and I think he'd make a damn good director
mself. Right from the start he knew what we
tended the role to be about. He had just the right
winkle, the right amount of authority. We wanted a
ero, and Connery's a hero."

nd so to *Outland*, an enormously successful original
creenplay by its director Peter Hyams, and a
haracter arguably closer to the real Sean Connery
an anything he has played before: a rugged and
utspoken individualist. Connery says: "It's one of
he first space films I've seen where I could
nderstand what it was all about without getting into
ll those jet packs and ray guns and what have you.
tar Wars and *The Empire Strikes Back* were a
omplete mystery to me. I was drawn to it because it
vas about a man on his own particular odyssey. Alone
gainst the system." Says director Peter Hyams (who
lso made the brilliant and underrated *Capricorn
One*): "The film is about a man who has reached a
oint in his life where he draws the line, where he sees
wrong and feels a responsibility to stand up to it. A
tubborn man. A decent man. A man with a sense of
trength as well as intelligence and vulnerability."
About his leading man, Hyams said: "Sean has a very
owerful image on screen and he's a tremendous
raftsman. His emotions seem so very close to the
urface of the skin that when you see him on screen,
ou can truly sense what he's feeling. It's an
normous asset for a fine actor."

Connery plays Marshal O'Neil, a policeman of the
uture, who arrives at the mining base on Io, a moon

*Opposite: in
Diamonds are
Forever*

of Jupiter, to find that the titanium mine worke·
have been breaking all records there — and going o·
of their minds in the process. The reason is a massi·
drug racket which O'Neil decides to halt. Many criti·
welcomed *Outland* as *High Noon* in space as O'Ne·
plays cat and mouse with the hired killers mining bo·
Sheppard (Peter Boyle) sends for to deal with O'Nei·
The film moves towards an unbearably tense clim·
as O'Neil stands alone against the system — and th·
only hand of friendship comes from a sassy doct·
(marvellously played by Frances Sternhagen).

After *Outlaw* Connery made *Wrong is Right* f·
director Richard Brooks, also starring Hardy Kruge·
John Saxon, Robert Webber, Katharine Ross,·
contemporary black comedy involving the escapad·
of a troubleshooting international journali·
(Connery).

With scarcely a break he went to Switzerland to begi·
work with veteran Fred Zinnemann on *Maide·

Opposite: with Ian Bannen in Sidney Lumet's The Offence

Below: with Daniela Bianchi in From Russia with Love

Maiden (working title) which Connery describes as "a small story with an epic quality." Based on a short story by Kay Boyle it tells the bitter sweet love story of a young Scottish girl (newcomer Betsy Brantley) and a married doctor 25 years her senior (Connery). During a climbing holiday in the Alps the desparity in their ages becomes the subject of gossip and a handsome young guide (Lambert Wilson) comes between them. The moment of truth is reached when the rivals challenge a particularly hazardous peak known as the Maiden. As Connery — who had never climbed mountains before — commented wryly: "It was dangerous work — the sun kept melting the ice, making the crevasses treacherous. Fortunately we had eight of the world's best climbers working on it." Zinnemann once defined his idea of happiness as "being on top of the Matterhorn wondering how to get down," so airlifting 130 cast and crew 8,000 ft on to the face of a glacier in the Swiss Alps for three days

Opposite: in The Offence

Below: with Claudine Auger and Adolfo Celi in Thunderball

filming must have seemed close to his ideal of happiness.

Sean Connery is an ambitious man and a realistic one. "I don't think anyone doing anything creative is ever completely satisfied," he says. "By the time an old project appears you're deep in the problems of new ones — and when you do see the earlier thing, its weaknesses stare you in the face. I have no illusions that anything I'm going to do will give me complete satisfaction." When he shed the skin of James Bond he knew he was gambling ("Other people said I was crazy, but I've always thought that to quit was right for me") but he does not rule out the possibility of playing Bond again. A few years ago he worked on a new Bond script with writer Len Deighton, but backed off when quarrels started about rights. "The lawyers started crawling out of the woodwork and I thought enough was enough." Now that John Gardner has written "Licence Renewed" the speculation has rekindled.

Opposite: in Zardoz

Below: with Richard Harris in The Molly Maguires

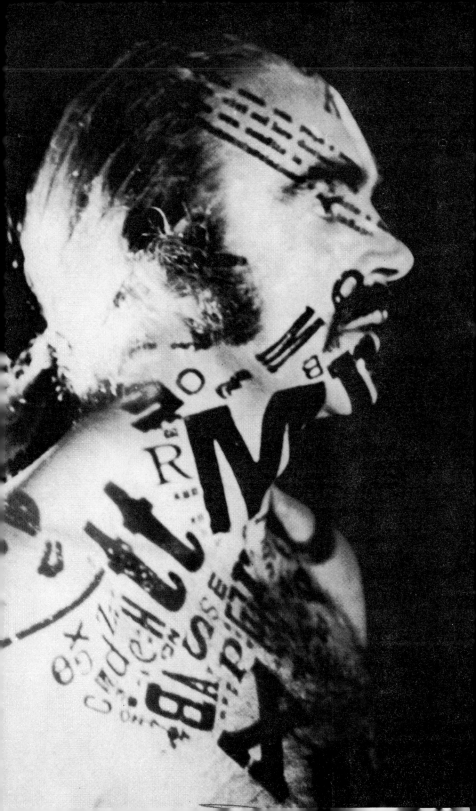

He became an actor almost by accident in the beginning, certainly not out of any consuming passion for acting. That he stays an actor is a measure of how well he has succeeded, for Connery is doggedly determined and would never continue in a profession that was not rewarding. "I may not be qualified to be an actor," he says, "But I'm certainly not qualified to be anything else."

The discipline of acting he accepts. He stopped smoking several years ago and tries not to drink too much. He is a man of few words, sombre and not given to frivolous pleasantries, but when he is talking about something that interests him — like the Scottish Trust, some of his films and always, obsessively, golf — he almost gets carried away by his own enthusiasms. The days of James Bond may have taken their toll, but Connery has emerged professionally and personally unscathed.

Opposite: with Charlotte Rampling in Zardoz

Below: with Jill St John in Diamonds are Forever

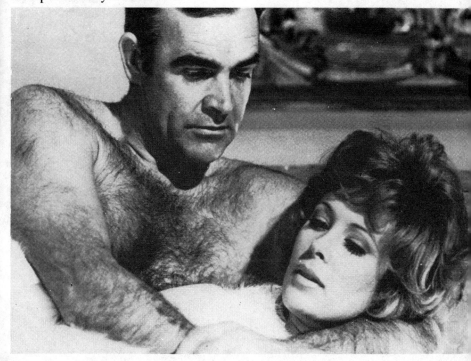

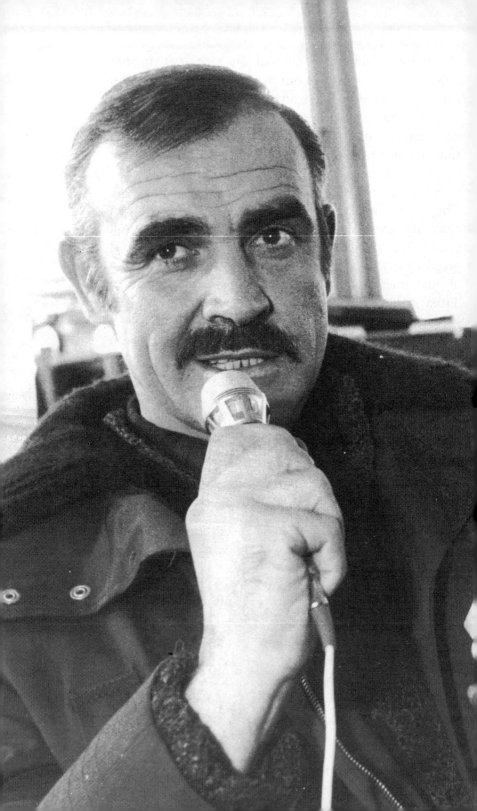

NO ROAD BACK (GB 1956)

Prod/Steve Pallos. Dir/Montgomery Tully. Scr/Charles A Leeds, Montgomery Tully. Music/John Veale. Ph/Lionel Banes. B&W. GB distribution/RKO-Radio. Certificate A. 83 mins.

With: Skip Homeier (John Railton), Paul Carpenter (Clem Hayes), Patricia Dainton (Beth), Norman Woodland (Inspector Harris), Margaret Rawlings (Mrs Railton), Eleanor Summerfield (Marguerite), Alfie Bass (Rudge Harvey), Sean Connery (Spike)

This little thriller in which Connery made his début film appearance starred Margaret Rawlings as Mrs Railton, a blind and deaf lady who acted as a fence for the criminals who used her London club as their base. Connery played Spike, one of the gang members.

HELL DRIVERS (GB 1957)

Prod/S Benjamin Fisz. Dir/C Raker Endfield (Cy Endfield). Scr/John Kruse, C Raker Endfield. Music/Hubert Clifford. Ph/Geoffrey Unsworth. B&W. GB distribution/Rank. Certificate A. 108 mins.

With: Stanley Baker (Tom), Herbert Lom (Gino), Peggy Cummins (Lucy), Patrick McGoohan (Red), William Hartnell (Cartley), Wilfred Lawson (Ed), Sidney James (Dusty), Jill Ireland (Jill), Alfie Bass (Tinker), Gordon Jackson (Scottie), Sean Connery (Johnny), Vera Day (Blonde)

Using lorries driven by the actors themselves, this was a story depicting the dangerous conditions under which truck drivers employed by a particular cheapjack road haulage company had to work. Connery appeared as Johnny — truck driver number 19.

TIME LOCK (GB 1957)

Prod/Peter Rogers. Dir/Gerald Thomas. Scr/Peter Rogers. Music/Stanley Black. Ph/Peter Hennessy. B&W. GB distribution/British Lion. Certificate A. 73 mins.

With: Robert Beatty (Dawson), Betty McDowall (Lucille Walker), Vincent Winter (Steven Walker), Lee Patterson (Colin Walker), Sandra Francis (Evelyn Webb), Alan Gifford (George Foster), Robert Ayres (Inspector Andrews), Victor Wood (Howard Zeeder), Jack Cunningham (Max Jarvis). *Sean Connery unbilled*

Connery was billed as "2nd welder" in this drama about a

Opposite: in Caspar Wrede's Ransom

mother (Betty McDowall) who goes with her young son (Vincent Winter) to pick her husband (Lee Patterson) up from work at a local bank branch. Just as the bank is about to close for the weekend, the boy accidentally gets locked in one of the vaults. With only between six and ten hours of oxygen left in the vault, it becomes a race against time to rescue him.

ACTION OF THE TIGER (GB 1957)

Prod/Kenneth Harper. Dir/Terence Young. Scr/Robert Carson. Music/Humphrey Searle. Ph/Desmond Dickinson. Technicolor. GB distribution/CIC (MGM). Certificate U. 93 mins.

With: Van Johnson (Carson), Martine Carol (Tracy), Herbert Lom (Trifon), Gustavo Rocco (Henri), Tony Dawson (Security officer), Anna Gerber (Mara), Yvonne Warren (Katina), Helen Hayes (Countess), Sean Connery (Mike)

Carson (Van Johnson) is an American runner of contraband approached in Athens by Tracy (Martine Carol), a French woman who wants him to help rescue her brother Henri from Albania where he is being kept a political prisoner.

ANOTHER TIME, ANOTHER PLACE (GB 1958)

Prod/Lewis Allen, Smedley Aston. Dir/Lewis Allen. Scr/ Stanley Mann. Music/Douglas Gamley. Ph/Jack Hildyard. B&W. GB distribution/CIC (Paramount). Certificate A. 95 mins.

With: Lana Turner (Sara Scott), Barry Sullivan (Carter Reynolds), Glynis Johns (Kay Trevor), Sean Connery (Mark Trevor), Sidney James (Jake Klein), Terence Longdon (Alan Thompson), Doris Hare (Mrs Bunker)

During World War II a female American journalist (Lana Turner) has an affair with a British BBC war correspondent (Connery). When he is killed in action, she goes to his home town to console his wife (Glynis Johns).

DARBY O'GILL & THE LITTLE PEOPLE (US 1959)

Prod/Walt Disney. Dir/Robert Stevenson. Scr/Lawrence Edward Watkin. Music/Oliver Wallis. Ph/Winton C Hoch. Technicolor. GB distribution/Walt Disney. Certificate U. 90 mins.

With: Albert Sharpe (Darby O'Gill), Jimmy O'Dea (King Brian), Janet Munro (Katie), Sean Connery (Michael McBride), Kieron Moore (Pony Sugme), Estelle Winwood

Opposite: in the all-star cast of Murder on the Orient Express

Sheelah), Walter Fitzgerald (Lord Fitzpatrick), Dennis O'Dea (Father Murphy), J G Devlin (Tom Kerrigan)

Based on H T Kavanagh's "Darby O'Gill" stories, this had Irish caretaker Darby O'Gill being kicked by his horse into an old well where he confronts King Brian, monarch of all the little people". O'Gill later captures the King and uses his magic powers to allow himself three wishes to rearrange his life. Connery played Michael McBride, assigned the task of taking over from O'Gill who is about to be retired.

TARZAN'S GREATEST ADVENTURE (GB 1959)

Prod/Sy Weintraub. Dir/John Guillermin. Scr/Berne Giler, John Guillerman. Ph/Skeets Kelly. GB distribution Paramount). Certificate U. 84 mins.

With: Gordon Scott (Tarzan), Anthony Quayle (Slade), Sara Shane (Angie), Sean Connery (O'Bannion), Niall MacGinnis (Kruger), Scilla Gabel (Tony), Al Mulock (Dino)

When four villainous diamond robbers are responsible for murdering several natives on an African settlement, Tarzan decides to pursue them and bring the gang to justice. Connery was cast as Dan O'Bannion, one of the baddies led by evil killer Slade (Anthony Quayle).

THE FRIGHTENED CITY (GB 1961)

Prod/John Lemont, Leigh Vance. Dir/John Lemont. Scr/ Leigh Vance. Music/Norrie Paramor. Ph/Desmond Dickinson. B&W. GB distribution/EMI. Certificate A. 98 mins.

With: Herbert Lom (Waldo Zhernikov), John Gregson (Sayers), Sean Connery (Paddy Damion), Alfred Marks (Harry Foulcher), Yvonne Romain (Anya), Olive McFarland (Sadie), Kenneth Griffiths (Wally)

When a crooked accountant (Herbert Lom) hits upon the idea of amalgamating the six main gangs that run London's protection racket into one syndicate, all goes according to plan until one of the gangs decide to return to being independent. As Paddy Damion, Connery played a burglar engaged to collect the money, but who turns against the organisation when a friend is killed.

ON THE FIDDLE (US: OPERATION SNAFU) (GB 1961)

Prod/S Benjamin Fisz. Dir/Cyril Frankel. Scr/Harold Buchman. Music/Malcolm Arnold. Ph/Edward Scaife. B&W. GB distribution/EMI. Certificate A. 97 mins.

Opposite: in Murder on the Orient Express

With: Sean Connery (Pedlar Pascoe), Alfred Lynch (Horac
Pope), Cecil Parker (GP/CPT Bascombe), Wilfred Hyd
White (Trowbridge), Stanley Holloway (Cooksley)
Kathleen Harrison (Mrs Cooksley), Eleanor Summerfiel
(Flora McCaughton)

Alfred Lynch played a Cockney spiv to Connery
slow-witted gypsy in this comedy about two RAF serviceme
operating a lucrative racket which they hope will enable ther
to dodge field combat in warhit Europe.

THE LONGEST DAY (US 1962)

Prod/Darryl F Zanuck. Dir/Ken Annakin (British Exteriors)
Andrew Marton (American exteriors), Bernhard Wick
(German scenes), Darryl F Zanuck (American interiors)
Scr/Cornelius Ryan, based on his book. Music/Mauric
Jarre. Ph/Walter Wottitz. B&W. GB distribution/20t
Century-Fox. Certificate A. 108 mins.

With: Richard Burton (RAF pilot), Kenneth More (Cap
Maud), Peter Lawford (Lord Lovat), Richard Todd (Majo
Howard), Leo Genn (Brig Gen Parker), Michael Medwir
(Pte Watney), Norman Rossington (Pte Clough), Johr
Robinson (Admiral Ramsey), Donald Houston (RAF pilot)
Trevor Reid (Gen Montgomery), John Wayne (Lt Co
Vandervoort) Robert Mitchum (Brig Gen Cota), Henry
Fonda (Brig Gen Roosevelt), Robert Ryan (Brig Ger
Gavin), Richard Beymer (Pte Schultz), Mel Ferrer (Majo
Gen Haines), Jeffrey Hunter (Sgt Fuller), Sal Mineo (Pte
Martini), Roddy McDowall (Pte Morris), Eddie Albert (Co
Newton), Edmond O'Brien (Gen Barton), Red Buttons (Pte
Steel), Henry Grace (Gen Eisenhower), Christian Marquanc
(Com Kieffer), Artletty (Mme Barrault), Madelein Renauc
(Mother Superior), Curt Jurgens (Major Gen Blumentritt).
Sean Connery unbilled

Complete with an all-star international cast, this acclaimec
recreation of the Allied invasion of Normandy in June 1944.
had Connery cast as Private Flanagan, a tough seasonec
veteran whose fighting spirit sees him through the landings at
Juno Beach.

DR. NO (GB 1962)

Prod/Harry Saltzman, Albert R Broccoli. Dir/Terence
Young. Scr/Richard Maibaum, Johanne Harwood, Berkely
Mather. Music/Monty Norman. GB distribution/
United Artists. Certificate A. 105 mins.

*Opposite:
between takes on
The Man Who
Would Be King*

With: Sean Connery (James Bond), Ursula Andress (Honey), Joseph Wiseman (Dr No), Jack Lord (Felix Leiter), Anthony Dawson (Prof Dent), John Kitzmiller (Quarrel), Zena Marshall (Miss Taro), Bernard Lee ("M"), Lois Maxwell (Miss Moneypenny), Eunice Gayson (Sylvia), Lester Prendergast (Puss-Feller)

The first of the 007 pictures, in which James Bond goes to Jamaica to investigate the mysterious death of a British agent, and inadvertently comes across some strange activities by Dr No (Joseph Wiseman). It transpires that the doctor is the possessor of a secret weapon which can destroy nearby space station, Cape Canaveral.

FROM RUSSIA WITH LOVE (GB 1963)

Prod/Harry Saltzman, Albert R Broccoli. Dir/Terence Young. Scr/Richard Maibaum, Johanne Harwood. Music/ John Barry. Ph/Ted Moore. Technicolor. GB distribution/ United Artists. Certificate A. 116 mins.

With: Sean Connery (James Bond), Daniela Bianchi (Tatiana Romanova), Pedro Armendariz (Kerim Bey), Lotte Lenya (Rosa Klebb), Robert Shaw (Red Grant), Bernard Lee ("M"), Eunice Gayson (Sylvia), Walter Gotell (Morzeny), Lois Maxwell (Miss Moneypenny), Francis de Wolff (Vavra), George Pastell (Train conductor), Nadja Regin (Kerim's girl), Aliza Gur (Vida), Martine Beswick (Zora), Vladek Sheybal (Kronsteen)

James Bond has been assigned to aid a young Russian girl, Tatiana Romanova, who wishes to defect from her job in the Russian Embassy in Istanbul. Trying to stop them is an international crime organisation called SPECTRE, who have hired ruthless killer Red Grant (Robert Shaw) to dispose of Bond and thus confound both the British and Russian secret service, while they devise a plan to steal a special coding machine.

WOMAN OF STRAW (GB 1964)

Prod/Michael Relph. Dir/Basil Dearden. Scr/Robert Muller, Stanley Mann, Michael Relph. Music/Muir Mathieson. Ph/ Otto Heller. Eastman Colour. GB distribution/United Artists. Certificate A. 117 mins.

With: Gina Lollobrigida (Maria), Sean Connery (Anthony Richmond), Ralph Richardson (Charles Richmond), Johnny Sekka (Thomas), Laurence Hardy (Baines), Danny Daniels (Fenton), Peter Madden (Captain), Alexander Knox (Lomer)

Opposite: in
The Man Who
Would Be King

Hating his rich and ruthless uncle Charles Richmond for driving his father to suicide, and knowing there is little chance of inheriting the business tycoon's vast fortune, nephew Anthony Richmond conspires with the household nurse Maria, to murder the old man.

MARNIE (US 1964)
Prod-dir/Alfred Hitchcock, Scr/Jay Presson Allen. Music/Bernard Herrmann. Ph/Robert Burks. Technicolor. GB distribution/Rank. Certificate X. 130 mins.
With: Sean Connery (Mark Rutland), Tippi Hedren (Marnie), Diane Baker (Lil Mainwaring), Martin Gabel (Sidney Strutt), Louis Latham (Bernice Edgar), Bob Sweeney (Cousin Bob), Alan Napier (Mr Rutland), S John Launer (Sam Ward), Mariette Hartley (Susan Claborn), Bruce Dern (Sailor)
Marnie is a kleptomaniac who wanders from town to town changing jobs. Each time, she convinces her employer of her reliability before making off with the contents of his safe. Her latest boss, Mark Rutland, falls in love with her and, in an effort to understand her illness, marries and cures her; but then has to help Marnie confront a nightmare in her past that still makes her sexually frigid.

GOLDFINGER (GB 1964)
Prod/Harry Saltzman, Albert R Broccoli, Dir/Guy Hamilton. Scr/Richard Maibaum, Paul Dehn. Music/John Barry. Ph/Ted Moore. GB distribution/United Artists. Certificate A. 109 mins.
With: Sean Connery (James Bond), Honor Blackman (Pussy Galore), Gert Frobe (Goldfinger), Shirley Eaton (Jill Masterson), Tania Mallet (Tilly Masterson), Harold Sakata (Odd Job), Bernard Lee ("M"), Martin Benson (Solo), Cec Linder (Felix Leiter), Austin Willis (Simmons), Lois Maxwell (Miss Moneypenny), Bill Nagy (Midnight), Alf Joint (Capungo)
Agent 007 is assigned to investigate the secret empire of Auric Goldfinger, one of the wealthiest men in the world. Bond subsequently learns of Goldfinger's audacious plan to rob America of its entire gold reserves, stored in the vaults of Fort Knox.

Opposite: with Audrey Hepburn in Robin and Marian

THE HILL (GB 1965)
Prod/Kenneth Hyman. Dir/Sidney Lumet. Scr/Ray Rigby.

Ph/Oswald Morris. B&W. GB distribution/CIC (MGM).
Certificate X. 123 mins.
With: Sean Connery (Joe Roberts), Harry Andrews (RSM
Wilson), Ian Bannen (Harris), Alfred Lynch (George
Stevens), Ossie Davis (Jacko King), Roy Kinnear (Monty
Bartlett), Jack Watson (Jock McGrath), Ian Hendry
(Williams), Michael Redgrave (Medical Officer), Norman
Bird (Commandant), Neil McCarthy (Burton), Howard
Goorney (Walters)
As one of the forms of punishment in a British military
stockade in North Africa during World War II, prisoners are
repeatedly forced to climb, in full fighting gear, an almost
sheer, man-made hill. The film depicts five such prisoners,
including Joe Roberts, court-martialed for striking another
officer, who are pushed to the very limits of human
endurance by sadistic Staff Sergeant Williams.

THUNDERBALL (US 1965)
Prod/Harry Saltzman, Albert R Broccoli. Dir/Terence
Young. Scr/Richard Maibaum, John Hopkins. Music/
John Barry. Ph/Ted Moore. Technicolor. GB distribution/
United Artists. Certificate A. 130 mins.
With: Sean Connery (James Bond), Claudine Auger
(Domino), Adolfo Celi (Largo), Luciana Paluzzi (Fiona),
Rik Van Nutter (Felix Leiter), Bernard Lee ("M"), Martine
Beswick (Paula), Guy Doleman (Count Lippe), Molly Peters
(Patricia), Desmond Llewelyn ("Q"), Lois Maxwell (Miss
Moneypenny)
Connery goes underwater in his fourth outing as 007, against
his old adversary, SPECTRE. This time the international
crime syndicate have stolen two atomic bombs which they
have hidden in a secret underwater cave. Holding the western
powers to ransom, they demand diamonds worth 100 million
pounds in return for the two warheads.

A FINE MADNESS (US 1966)
Prod/Jerome Hellman. Dir/Irvin Kershner. Scr/Elliott
Baker. Music/John Addison. Ph/Ted McCord. Technicolor.
GB distribution/Columbia-Warner (Warner). Certificate A.
104 mins.
With: Sean Connery (Samson Shillitoe), Joanne Woodward
(Rhonda), Jean Seberg (Lydia West), Patrick O'Neal (Dr
Oliver West), Colleen Dewhurst (Dr Vera Kropotkin), Clive
Revill (Dr Menken), Werner Peters (Dr Vorbeck), John

Opposite: as Robin Hood in Dick Lester's Robin and Marian

Fielder (Daniel K Papp), Kay Medford (Mrs Fish), Jackie Coogan (Mr Fitzgerald)

Based on Elliott Baker's novel, this had Connery cast as Samson Shillitoe, a frustrated and rebellious poet living in New York, who is prone to outbursts of violence. Joanne Woodward appeared as the wife, trying to cope with her husband's unpredictable moods.

YOU ONLY LIVE TWICE (GB 1967)

Prod/Harry Saltzman, Albert R Broccoli. Dir/Lewis Gilbert. Scr/Ronald Dahl. Music/John Barry. Ph/Freddie Young. Technicolor. GB distribution/United Artists. Certificate A. 116 mins.

With: Sean Connery (James Bond), Aikiko Wakabayashi (Aki), Tetsuro Tamba (Tiger Tanaka), Mie Hama (Kissy Suzaki), Teru Shimada (Osato), Karin dor (Helga Brandt), Lois Maxwell (Miss Moneypenny), Desmond Llewelyn ("Q"), Bernard Lee ("M"), Charles Gray (Henderson), Tsai Chin (Chinese Girl), Donald Pleasence (Blofeld), Alexander Knox (American President), Robert Hutton (President's aide)

War between Russia and the United States seems imminent when both countries accuse the other of trying to sabotage their space projects. British intelligence, however, believes that the interfering rockets are being launched by an outside power from somewhere in Japan. James Bond is sent there to investigate further.

SHALAKO (GB 1968)

Prod/Euan Lloyd. Dir/Edward Dmytryk. Scr/J J Griffith, Hal Hopper, Scott Finch. Music/Robert Farnon. Ph/Ted Moore. Technicolor. GB distribution/Columbia-Warner (Warner). Certificate A. 113 mins.

With: Sean Connery (Shalako), Brigitte Bardot (Irina Lazaar), Stephen Boyd (Bosky Fulton), Jack Hawkins (Sir Charles Daggett), Peter Van Eyck (Frederick von Hallstatt), Honor Blackman (Lady Daggett), Woody Strode (Chato), Eric Sykes (Mako), Alexander Knox (Henry Clarke)

In his only western to date, Connery played a cowboy engaged as a guide for European artistocratic big game hunters. But, as the party shoots its way across New Mexico, surrounding Indians become incensed and attack them.

Opposite: in A Bridge Too Far

THE MOLLY MAGUIRES (US 1969)

Prod-dir/Martin Ritt. Scr/Walter Bernstein. Music/Henry Mancini. Ph/James Wong Howe. Technicolor. GB distribution/CIC (Paramount). Certificate A. 125 mins.

With: Richard Harris (James McParlan), Sean Connery (Jack Kehoe), Samantha Eggar (Mary Raines), Frank Finlay (Captain Davies), Anthony Zerbe (Dougherty), Bethel Leslie (Mrs Kehoe), Art Lund (Frazier), Anthony Costello (Frank McAndrew)

Set in Pennsylvania during 1876, the Molly Maguires are a secret organisation formed by Jack Kehoe and his men, aimed at making life difficult for mining officials as a protest against the hard and brutal working conditions to which they are subjected. The mine owners retaliate by sending in undercover detective James McParlan to infiltrate the group and relay back forthcoming troubles. Despite the friendship that forms between Kehoe and McParlan, ultimate betrayal is inevitable.

LA TENDA ROSSA (GB: THE RED TENT) (Italy/USSR 1969)

Prod/Franco Cristaldi. Dir/Mikhail K Kalatozov. Scr/Ennio De Concini, Richard Adams. Music/Ennio Morricone. Ph/Leonid Kalashnikov. Technicolor, GB distribution/CIC (Paramount). Certificate U. 121 mins.

With: Peter Finch (General Nobile), Sean Connery (Amundsen), Claudia Cardinale (Valeria), Hardy Kruger (Lundborg), Mario Adorf (Biagi), Massimo Girotti (Romangna), Luigi Vannucchi (Zappi), Edward Marzevic (Malmgren)

This is the story of General Nobile's ill-fated 1928 expedition by dirigible to the Arctic. When disaster struck and it crashed, Nobile was the first to be rescued, and afterwards was accused of abandoning his comrades. Connery appeared as Roald Amundsen, the Norwegian explorer who lost his life in an attempt to rescue the survivors.

THE ANDERSON TAPES (US 1971)

Prod/Robert M Weitman. Dir/Sidney Lumet. Scr/Frank R Pierson. Music/Quincy Jones. Ph/Arthur J Ornitz. Technicolor. GB distribution/Columbia-Warner (Columbia). Certificate AA. 99 mins.

With: Sean Connery (Duke Anderson), Dyan Cannon (Ingrid Everleigh), Martin Balsam (Tommy Haskins), Ralph Meeker (Captain Delaney), Alan King (Pat Angelo),

Opposite: in A Bridge Too Far

Christopher Walken (The Kid), Val Avery (Socks Parelli), Dick Williams (Spencer)

Ex-convict Duke Anderson visits his old girl friend Ingrid Everleigh and finds that she lives in a building that is a haven for luxurious apartments inhabited by the wealthy. He subsequently forms a gang to help him rob all the apartments, not knowing that the place is bugged by the police who are tape-recording all his conversations.

DIAMONDS ARE FOREVER (GB 1971)

Prod/Harry Saltzman, Albert R Broccoli. Dir/Guy Hamilton. Scr/Richard Maibaum, Tom Mankiewicz. Music/ John Barry. Ph/Ted Moore. Technicolor. GB distribution/ United Artists. Certificate A. 120 mins.

With: Sean Connery (James Bond), Jill St John (Tiffany Case), Charles Gray (Blofeld), Lana Wood (Plenty O'Toole), Jimmy Dean (Willard Whyte), Bruce Cabot (Saxby), Putty Smith (Mr Kidd), Bruce Glover (Mr Wint), Norman Burton (Leiter), Joseph Furst (Dr Metz), Bernard Lee ("M"), Desmond Llewelyn ("Q"), Lois Maxwell (Miss Moneypenny), Leonard Barr (Shady Tree)

Connery's final(?) appearance as James Bond found him investigating a diamond smuggling racket, with adventures in Amsterdam, a Los Angeles crematorium, various Las Vegas casinos, and finally a secret desert installation.

THE OFFENCE (GB 1972)

Prod/Denis O'Dell. Dir/Sidney Lumet. Scr/John Hopkins. Music/Harris Birtwhistle. GB distribution/United Artists. Certificate X. 113 mins.

With: Sean Connery (Johnson), Trevor Howard (Cartwright), Vivien Merchant (Maureen), Ian Bannen (Baxter), Derek Newark (Jessard), John Hallam (Panton), Peter Bowles (Cameron), Ronald Radd (Lawson), Anthony Sagar (Hill), Howard Goorney (Lambeth), Richard Moore (Garrett), Maxine Gordon (Janie)

Of all his films, Sidney Lumet's remains Connery's personal favourite. He played a tough policeman who suffers a gradual breakdown after twenty years in the force. When a suspected child molester dies under his ruthless interrogation, Johnson painfully discovers that he is no longer immune to the criminality he has witnessed over the years.

Opposite: in
The First Great
Train Robbery

ZARDOZ (GB 1973)

Prod-dir-scr/John Boorman. Music/David Munrow. Ph/ Geoffrey Unsworth. Colour by Deluxe. GB distribution/ Fox-Rank. Certificate X. 106 mins (GB:105 mins).

With: Sean Connery (Zed), Charlotte Rampling (Consuella), Sara Kestelman (Kay), Sally Anne Newton (Avalow), John Alderton (Friend), Niall Buggy (Arthur Frayn), Bosco Hogan (George Saden), Jessica Swift (A pathetic), Bairbre Dowling (Star), Christopher Casson (Old Scientist), Reginald Jarman (Death)

John Boorman's film is set in the year 2293. Most of the action takes place in what is known as the Vortex, a technological commune whose members have discovered the secret of eternal life. Protected by a force field, they are sealed off from a desolated world beyond their confine, but Zed (Connery), a mysterious outsider, penetrates their carefully guarded seclusion, forcing a dramatic confrontation with those inside.

RANSOM (GB 1974)

Prod/Peter Rawley. Dir/Casper Wrede. Scr/Paul Wheeler. Music/Jerry Goldsmith. Ph/Sven Nykvist. Eastman Colour. GB distribution/British Lion. Certificate A. 98 mins.

With: Sean Connery (Nils Tahlivik), Ian McShane (Petrie), Norman Bristow (Captain Denver), John Cording (Bert), Isabel Dean (Mrs Palmer), William Fox (Ferris), Richard Hampton (Joe), Robert Harris (Palmer), Harry Landis (Lookout pilot), Preston Lockwood (Hislop), James Maxwell (Bernard), John Quentin (Shepherd), Jeffrey Wickham (Barnes)

The British Ambassador to Scandinavia is kidnapped by terrorists demanding the release of six prisoners held in an English jail, plus a Boeing as a means of escape. Connery, as head of Norwegian security, is determined that the terrorists will not succeed.

MURDER ON THE ORIENT EXPRESS (GB 1974)

Prod/John Bradbourne, Richard Goodwin. Dir/Sidney Lumet. Scr/Paul Dehn. Music/Richard Rodney Bennet. Ph/ Geoffrey Unsworth. Technicolor. GB distribution/EMI. Certificate A. 131 mins.

With: Albert Finney (Hercule Poirot), Lauren Bacall (Mrs Hubbard), Martin Balsam (Bianchi), Ingrid Bergman (Greta), Jacqueline Bisset (Countess Andrenyi), Jean-Pierre

Opposite: in
The First Great
Train Robbery

Cassel (Pierre), Sean Connery (Col. Arbuthnott), John Gielgud (Beddoes), Wendy Hiller (Princess Dragomiroff), Anthony Perkins (McQueen), Vanessa Redgrave (Mary Debenham), Rachel Roberts (Hildegarde), Richard Widmark (Ratchett), Michael York (Count Andrenyi)

Albert Finney was virtually unrecognisable in his make-up as super-sleuth Hercule Poirot, in this all-star production of Agatha Christie's whodunit, set in the 1930s. Connery played the brusque Colonel Arbuthnot, one of twelve suspects in the case of a murder, committed aboard the Orient Express, snowbound on its way to the Yugoslav frontier.

THE WIND AND THE LION (US 1975)

Prod/Herb Jaffe. Dir-scr/John Milius. Music/Jerry Goldsmith. Ph/Billy Williams. Metrocolor. GB distribution/ Columbia-Warner (Columbia). Certificate A. 119 mins.

With: Sean Connery (Mulay El Raisuli), Candice Bergen (Eden Pedecaris), Brian Keith (Theodore Roosevelt), John Huston (John Hay), Geoffrey Lewis (Gummere), Steve Kanaly (Captain Jerome), Roy Jenson (Admiral Chadwick), Vladek Sheybal (Bashaw)

In turn-of-the-century Tangier, American widow Mrs Eden Pedecaris and her two children are taken captive by a bandit called Raisuli. Outraged by the kidnapping, but viewing the incident as an opportunity to make headlines and attract votes in the coming election, US president Theodore Roosevelt becomes involved in the rescue attempt.

THE MAN WHO WOULD BE KING (US 1975)

Prod/John Foreman. Dir/John Huston. Scr/John Huston, Gladys Hill. Music/Maurice Jarre. Ph/Oswald Morris. Colour. GB distribution/Columbia-Warner (Columbia). Certificate A. 129 mins.

With: Sean Connery (Daniel Dravot), Michael Caine (Peachy Carnehan), Christopher Plummer (Rudyard Kipling), Saeed Jaffrey (Billy Fish), Karroum Ben Bouih (Kafu Selim), Jack May (District Commissioner), Doghmi Larbi (Ootah), Shakira Caine (Roxanne)

As Dravot, the rascally ex-British Army Sergeant who manages to convince a remote colony of people in India that he's a God, Connery complemented perfectly the casting of Michael Caine as his fellow officer and companion, in John Huston's masterly screen version of the Rudyard Kipling adventure.

Opposite: in Cuba

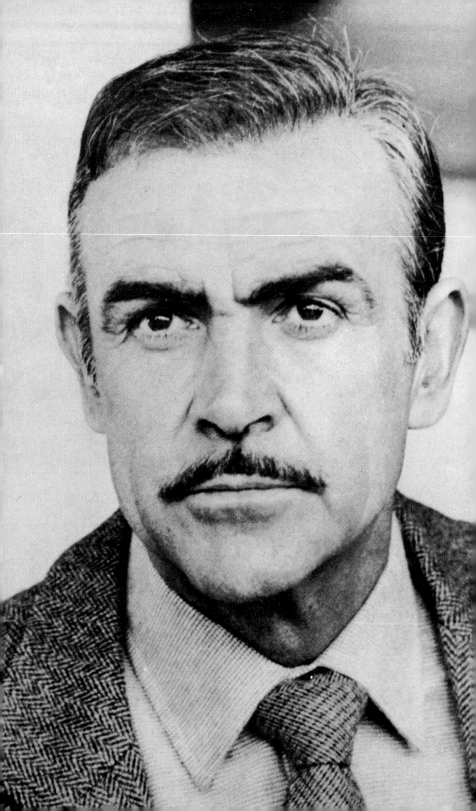

ROBIN AND MARIAN (US 1976)

Prod/Denis O'Dell. Dir/Richard Lester. Music/John Barry. Scr/James Goldman. Ph/David Watkin. Colour. GB distribution/Columbia-Warner (Columbia). Certificate A. 107 mins.

With: Sean Connery (Robin Hood), Audrey Hepburn (Maid Marian), Robert Shaw (Sheriff of Nottingham), Richard Harris (King Richard), Nicol Williamson (Little John), Denholm Elliott (Will Scarlett), Kenneth Haigh (Sir Ranulf)
An ageing Robin Hood returns to Sherwood Forest after fighting in the Crusades, and rekindles his romance with Maid Marian. He also attempts finally to conquer his arch-enemy, the Sheriff of Nottingham.

THE NEXT MAN (US 1976)

Prod/Martin Bregman. Dir/Richard C Sarafian. Scr/Mort Fine, Alan R Trustman, David M Wolf, Richard C Sarafian. Music/Michael Kamen. Ph/Michael Chapman. Technicolor. GB distribution/Harris Films. 107 mins.

With: Sean Connery (Hamid Abdul-Muhsen), Cornelia Sharpe (Nicole Scott), Albert Paulsen (Hamid), Adolfo Celi (Al Sharif), Marco St John (Justin), Ted Beniades (Frank Dedario)
Suave professional assassin Nicole Scott is hired to kill Khalil Abdul-Muhsen, the Saudi Arabian Minister of State, due to deliver a speech at a United Nations congress. Her task is made more difficult when she discovers that she is in love with the Arab peacemaker, following an intimate weekend in the Bahamas where she had planned to make her killing.

A BRIDGE TOO FAR (US 1977)

Prod/Joseph E Levine, Richard P Levine, Dir/Richard Attenborough. Scr/William Goldman. Music/John Addison. Ph/Geoffrey Unsworth. Eastman Colour. GB distribution/ United Artists. Certificate A. 175 mins.

With: Dirk Bogarde (Lt Gen Browning), James Caan (Sgt Eddie Dohun), Michael Caine (Lt Col Joe Vandeleur), Sean Connery (Maj Gen Urquhart), Elliot Gould (Col Bobby Stout), Gene Hackman (Maj Gen Sosabowski), Anthony Hopkins (Lt Col Frost), Hardy Kruger (Gen Ludwig), Laurence Olivier (Dr Spaander), Ryan O'Neal (Brig Gen Gavin), Robert Redford (Maj Julian Cook), Maximilian Schell (Lt Gen Bittrich), Liv Ullmann (Kate ter Horst)
Adding his illustrious name to a cast of other superstars,

Opposite: in Cuba

Connery appeared as Major-General Roy Urquhart, making his first ever combat airdrop in Operation Market Garden — the plan that led to a disastrous defeat for the Allied army at the battle of Arnhem in September 1944.

THE FIRST GREAT TRAIN ROBBERY (GB 1978)

Prod/John Foreman. Dir-scr/Michael Crichton, based on his novel. Music/Jerry Goldsmith. Ph/Geoffrey Unsworth. Technicolor. GB distribution/United Artists. Certificate AA. 108 mins.

With: Sean Connery (Edward Pierce), Donald Sutherland (Agar), Lesley-Anne Down (Miriam), Alan Webb (Edgar Trent), Malcolm Terris (Henry Fowler), Robert Lang (Detective Sharp)

In 1885, elegant crook Edward Pierce enlists the aid of his friend Agar (an expert in picking pockets and locks) and mistress Miriam, to help him in a daring attempt to rob a moving train of its gold bullion. Michael Crichton's witty comedy thriller had Connery doing all his own stunts, including the perilous scenes on top of the speeding train.

METEOR (US 1979)

Prod/Arnold Orgolini, Theodore Parvin. Dir/Ronald Neame. Scr/Stanley Mann, Edmund H North. Music/Laurence Rosenthal. Ph/Paul Lohmann. Colour by Movielab. GB distribution/Columbia-EMI-Warner (Warner). Certificate A. 107 mins.

With. Sean Connery (Dr Paul Bradley), Natalie Wood (Tatiana Donskaya), Karl Malden (Harry Sherwood), Brian Keith (Dr Dubov), Martin Landau (General Adlon), Trevor Howard (Sir Michael Hughes), Henry Fonda (The President)

The story deals with an attempt by American and Russian scientists to divert an imminent collision with Earth of a huge meteor hurtling towards the planet. Advance fragments of the meteor have already destroyed much of New York. As America's leading astrophysicist, Connery is called upon to work with a top Russian scientist, Natalie Wood, to change the course of the meteor.

CUBA (US 1979)

Prod/Alex Winitsky, Arlene Sellers. Dir/Richard Lester. Scr/Charles Wood. Music/Patrick Williams. Ph/David Watkin. Technicolor. GB distribution/United Artists. Certificate AA. 122 mins.

Opposite: in
Time Bandits

With: Sean Connery (Major Robert Dapes), Brooke Adams (Alexandra Pulido), Jack Weston (Gutman), Denholm Elliott (Skinner), Martin Balsam (General Bello), Chris Sarandon (Juan Pulido)

During the last few weeks of the ailing Batista regime in Cuba, Briton Robert Dapes arrives in Havana where he meets old flame Alexandra Pulido, now married to a playboy who takes her love for granted. Amid the tumultuous beginnings of the Castro revolution, Dapes tries to persuade Alexandra to leave the country with him.

TIME BANDITS (GB 1981)

Prod-dir/Terry Gilliam. Scr/Michael Palin, Terry Gilliam. Music/Mike Moran. Ph/Peter Biziou. Technicolor. GB distribution/Handmade Films. Certificate A. 113 min.

With: John Cleese (Robin Hood), Sean Connery (King Agamemnon), Shelley Duvall (Pansy), Katherine Helmond (Mrs Ogre), Ian Holm (Napoleon), Michael Palin (Vincent), Ralph Richardson (Supreme Being), Peter Vaughn (Ogre), David Warner (Evil Genius)

A conclave of dwarfs and their reluctant young companion, Kevin, time-trip through the holes left in the fabric of the universe by an over-ambitious Supreme Being forced into creating the world in only six days. Connery made a cameo appearance as King Agamemnon in an episode set in ancient Greece.

OUTLAND (GB 1981)

Prod/Richard A Roth. Dir-scr/Peter Hyams. Music/Jerry Goldsmith. Ph/Steven Goldblatt. Technicolor. GB

Opposite: in Outland

Below: Bond gatecrashes an astronaut training ground in Diamonds are Forever

distribution/Columbia-EMI-Warner (Warner). Certificate AA. 109 mins.

With: Sean Connery (William T O'Niel), Peter Boyle (Sheppard), Frances Sternhagen (Dr Lazarus), James B Sikking (Montone), Kika Markham (Carol), Clarke Peters (Ballard)

In Peter Hyam's galactic re-working of the western, *High Noon*, Connery plays a federal marshal forced to fight a lone battle against drug smugglers operating in a mining colony stationed in outer space.

WRONG IS RIGHT (US 1981)

Prod/Ray Stark. Dir-scr/Richard Brooks.

With: Sean Connery, Hardy Kruger, John Saxon, Robert Webber, Katharine Ross, Robert Conrad, Henry Silva, Ron Moody, G D Spradlin

MAIDEN, MAIDEN (US 1981)

Prod-dir/Fred Zinnemann. Scr/Michael Austin. Ph/Giuseppe Rotunno. Colour. GB distribution/Columbia-EMI-Warner (Warner).

With: Sean Connery, Lambert Wilson, Betsy Brantley.

Set in 1932, the story is that of a love affair between a young girl (Brantley) and married doctor (Connery) whose relationship is threatened during a climbing holiday, when a handsome young guide comes between them. The rivalry between the two men reaches a climax when they both challenge a particularly hazardous peak known as the Maiden.

Opposite: in Outland

Below: with Vanessa Redgrave in Murder on the Orient Express